Manipulation through Persuasion

By

Alek Grigorov

Manipulation through Persuasion

Contents

Foreword

What is Power? How can I measure it? How much Power do I have? How can I gain greater Power? These are just a few questions that people from all ages have tried to *find* the *answers* to for centuries now and there is one possible answer that most of them miss.

From the dawn of time when the human *mind* began to *develop*, men and women have been battling over *gaining* this elusive sense of *Power* by making other people *accept* their ideas and *suggestions*. If you can *make* other *people agree* with your proposed ideas and they *take action* in accordance with your ideas, then it is safe to say you have gained some edge over them since *you have* used *an ability* that not that many people have developed to a high degree – the ability *to Influence*. The Power to *Persuade brings Satisfaction* not only to the one who is doing the influencing, but in most of the cases also to the person being influenced.

And what are the rewards to be gained from *learning* and *applying* the *skill to persuade*? Money, success, satisfaction, better life – whatever goal you set out to accomplish this useful and highly practical skill will aid you 100 %.

So, is it worth *becoming* more *Powerful* by *learning* and *applying* something that has always been highly valued? You decide and if you want to learn the *art of Persuasion*, delve into the story that will help you on your journey to living a more fulfilled life.

A.G.

Determined to Succeed

'What fools! If they would only listen! Their lives would unquestionably *become much better, richer, and happier* if they would only listen!' Arturo was very frustrated and disheartened while participating in this inner monologue that had enslaved his attention and energy. A young man of 20 Arturo Bonardi was very *ambitious* and *determined* to *become rich* by embarking on a journey across the world in hope of fulfilling his destiny to become a wealthy merchant. But there was one problem - nobody would really listen to Arturo's grand ideas and well-thought-out plans of travelling to unknown countries in search of proper commodities to trade. Even though he was very much a young man, he had spent years of studying at fine universities and travelling all over the world with his father on board numerous ships, always trading here and there and *making* small yet *consistent profits* and *having* the *discipline* to *save* all his *profits* and put them aside for greater things to come. But Arturo did not have the financial means to *become* a full time *successful* merchant on his own and that is why he was actively seeking out wealthy men and trying to persuade them to take a chance on him and multiply their investments if they would only give him a chance to prove his words. Of course, the wealthy men Arturo approached either directly laughed at the young man's proposals or they casually brushed him off without even bothering to give an explanation as to why they were reluctant to trust his ideas.

However, being the determined man he was brought up to be by his already late father, Arturo was not going to give up easily on his grandiose plans and dreams. He only needed to *learn* how *to convince other people* to trust him and accept his business proposals. And he knew just the man who could give him the desperately desired answers he was so frantically seeking that would make him into a man to be reckoned with.

The Man to Meet

Arturo's *desire for success* lead him to the Republic of Venice, where he was planning to meet and learn from the great master of the mercantile trade, who had *become* not only *wealthy* beyond measure, but also powerfully influential. Rulers from all of Europe would seek desperately the wise advice of this Venetian lord of the trade for he had amassed his riches not only through great knowledge and expertise in the field of trading, but also through his unusual ability to *communicate* seemingly *easily* and *effortlessly* with almost anyone and that had allowed him to *become* a *master persuader*, unlike the young Arturo, who even though had great plans combined with good intentions, was unable to get his ideas across the people of high status, whose help he so direly needed.

Arturo had heard various rumors and the most amazing stories about this great man of power they called Maurizio Maccarinelli. He did not know what exactly to believe, but he was utterly determined to make his acquaintance and by the powers of God he believed deeply in his heart he would do so.

That is why he saved enough money to finance his trip to Venice in hope of finding this great merchant and making a good impression on him. Once Arturo arrived in Venice he asked around for the nobleman's residence and about his daily routines and soon enough he learned that Signore Maccarinelli was a member of a most famous guild in the Republic.

On one beautiful sunny afternoon Arturo visited Signore Maccarinelli at his huge mansion to discuss business affairs with the great man. Arturo had spent weeks prior to that just trying to schedule an appointment with the ever-so-busy Venetian master of trade. Finally, the day had come for Arturo to meet Maurizio Maccarinelli, the man the whole of Venice owed so much since he had contributed immensely to the Republic's economic development for more than a decade. Arturo had prepared great lavish presents for Signore Maccarinelli as a sign of his gratitude for having accepted his request to meet with him – he presented his host with the most beautiful and priced silk from China. Arturo did everything in his power to look and act respectable before his famous host. He was very polite when addressing Signore Maccarinelli, but at one point in time the powerful Venetian increased the pressure by being very direct:

'I appreciate your gifts and your efforts to be very courteous. However, I am a busy man and I do not have time to waste. What is the actual purpose of your visit? What do you actually like to gain from this meeting?'

Arturo was taken aback from the bluntness of the merchant's words and he found himself instantly in a confused state of mind.

'I came here today to pay my respect to you Signore. You have been an inspiration to me for years now and I just wanted to let you know that you are the main reason why I got into the business of travelling the world and striving to *gain* financial *wealth* through trading various commodities. I was really hoping to *become* your *apprentice* and thus *learn directly* from you how to be a great merchant such as yourself and at the same time be as persuasive as you are famously known to be.'

Signore Maccarinelli's facial expression changed instantly – his cunning smile became apparent, his eyes fixated intensely on the young man as if admiring him and yet also at the same time studying him as a potential threat.

Dead silence. Anxiety started filling Arturo's whole body as he was sitting there quietly waiting for his host to say or do something that would break the unbearable tension that was building up by the second. And just when Arturo was on the verge of almost passing out due to his heart racing like a wild horse that had been scared by lightning, the silence was broken:

'**What is in it for me**?'

'What do you mean?' replied with apparent astoundment the young man.

'The first thing you need to *learn* in order *to* be able to *persuade* people is to know that every person you are trying to *influence* will have at the back of their mind this simple egoistical question that you have to tackle. Unless you can come up with a strategically well-planed-out answer to this unspoken question, you will fail to meet the other person's needs and they will be very reluctant to pay serious attention to what you have to offer to them. For you see, people in their primal nature are selfish and they are always on the lookout for obvious or hidden benefits that will *make them feel better*.'

'But that is the thing – I always come prepared and *list all* of the *benefits* that are in their *interest*, but for some reason people look at me as if I am lying to them. They smirk or tell me off as if I were a beggar or a charlatan. They will not even hear me out. That's why I really need your help, because everybody listens to you, everybody enjoys your company and they gladly accept your proposals. Can you help me be more like you?

'Again, I repeat – **What is in it for me**?' laughingly replied Signore Maccarinelli as to not only make a very strong point, but also to indicate that everything came with a price that had to be paid.

'I can give half of everything I make in the next 3 years as a payment for your vast knowledge and your agreeing to take me on as your apprentice.' uttered somehow anxiously the young Arturo with eyes full of hope and even of desperation shining through.

'Three fourths of everything you make till the day you perish is what I require for my tutelage.' pronounced ever so proudly and happily the elder merchant who knew he had caught himself a young fox and was already gloating from the fact that he was going to slowly skin the entrapped fox alive.

Arturo immediately felt his throat as dry as the sand in a hot desert, his stomach pierced by an invisible dagger and his knees on the verge of automatically shaking as a response to the merchant's devilish demand.

'I take your silence as a Yes. Come to my residence again tomorrow at dawn.' came down the sharp axe of the merciless executioner or at least that was the association that sprang up in Arturo's head when hearing the merchant deliver an imaginary yet at the same time very real sentence and a demand that allowed no objections.

The Manipulation has Begun

The very next day began terribly for Arturo. He could barely keep his eyes closed all through the night contemplating on the devious way in which he was *manipulated* into *obedience*. He could not wrap his mind around how exactly he had fallen prey to this old wolf who was going to take his time toying with his newfound victim and at the same time biting off cold bloodedly pieces of flesh. Chills ran down Arturo's spine while thinking of the mess he had put himself in, but there was no time for crying or whining or lamenting his destiny. There was only *time* and room *for action*, decisive action and Arturo realized it. After all, it was his own idea in the first place to attain the mentorship of the great Venetian and he had to follow through on his *commitment* for he had the *determination* of a slave to break the shackles of poverty and by God he was willing to do whatever it took to *become* a *master persuader* and turn his dream of a wealthy influential life into reality. That is why Arturo dressed well and with an *open, focused* and *eager, hungry mind* entered the premises of his host and teacher who was about to change his life forever.

Signore Maccarinelli welcomed back his apprentice with a wide and sincere smile that immediately put the young man at ease. He then extended his hand and shook Arturo's hand firmly, yet pleasantly while putting his other hand on the young man's shoulder. Arturo felt weird for he was feeling relaxed and at the same time could not get rid of the feeling that he was controlled, manipulated even.

'Come, young man, you have much to *learn* and I honestly admit that I even envy you a little.' spoke cordially the elder merchant.

'How come? Why would a wealthy and powerful man with high social status such as yourself feel envious of me Signore?' asked with bewilderment the young Arturo.

'Because you are still very much young and *energetic, eager to learn* and learn you shall. When I was your age, I would have given my left arm just to learn the knowledge you are about to get your hands, eyes and mind on. *Amassing knowledge* through years of hard experience *is* not fun – it's *essential*. However, digging for gold at the bountiful heart of a gold mine is not the same as trying to sieve and gather gold dust at a river. Come and brace yourself for once *your mind expands* after you *internalize* the *knowledge* you are to receive, it will never go back to its former shell.'

The Chest of Knowledge

Signore Maccarinelli went to a small hidden back room at the top floor of his mansion, where he kept his most prized possessions. He came of this hidden room with an ancient treasure chest that looked at least 300 years old and which had some strange and uncommon engravings and insignia on it. Arturo felt his heart start to race faster and faster at the sight of this treasure chest. The elder merchant's *keen observation skills* immediately caught the young man's changed body language and laughed heartily for a few seconds. Arturo felt embarrassed as if he was caught doing something wrong.

'I bet you would really want me to give you this here key that opens the treasure chest?' teasingly asked the Venetian holding a small key in his right hand.

'Signore, I am simply your humble apprentice and what you deem appropriate I will obey.' wittily answered the young man.

'Very good. Now you have to earn this key and before you can get your hands on it you need to do something first. Go to the marketplace and *persuade* the *people* you encounter there to tell you the name of the best goldsmith in Venice, but make sure you have the correct name without paying for this information. You have to *persuade them* to give you the name of the very best goldsmith for free and come back to me with that name. If you fail to obtain the name, I will have no other choice but to send you away. I'll give you one hint – when you talk to the people at the marketplace try to **be more like them**.'

'But why at the marketplace where there are numerous liars and scoundrels? Can't I just go to a guild and ask there?'

'No. You are missing the point. Do as I say – my servant will come with you to make sure you are not cheating.'

The Key is Within Reach

Arturo did exactly as he was told and even though it took hours of *persuasion* at the marketplace *and ingenuity* on his part, he was finally *convinced* he had obtained the name of the very best goldsmith in Venice and he hurriedly came back to the merchant's mansion.

'I have it.' proudly grinned Arturo.

'The name of the best goldsmith in Venice is Simone Battisti.'

'Very well. That is correct. Here is the key as promised.' gladly and deviously uttered Signore Maccarinelli.

Arturo rushed to open the chest with the key that was given to him and to his amazement and shock inside the chest the young man found another ancient and locked smaller chest. Signore Maccarinelli could not help but start laughing loudly at the surprised and at the same time disbelieving look that appeared on Arturo's face.

'You didn't think it was going to be that easy now did you?' the Venetian's voice mockingly broke the trance state the young man found himself in.

'I have a new assignment for you and as you might have already guessed – if you complete it successfully, you will receive the key to the second chest. Now *you have to persuade* the goldsmith to give you a very small amount of gold that would be enough for the making of a gold ring. You are to offer no money or merchandise in return for the gold and you need to bring the gold back to me within the next 3 hours.'

'But how would I do that?' asked Arturo.

'You have to **speak with passion**.' explained very cryptically the Venetian merchant.

One Key Closer

Arturo had to almost battle verbally with the best goldsmith in Venice for almost 2 hours before he finally obtained the gold that would complete the task he was sent to achieve. He *spoke with* so *much passion* and for so long that the old goldsmith finally broke down and gave the young man what he required. Arturo rushed back alongside the Venetian merchant's servant to get to Signore Maccarinelli's house on time. He felt his heart would explode from all of the running he was putting his body through, but his determination would not be denied, and he entered the rich man's mansion with just 2 minutes to spare.

'Right on time. Were you able to obtain what I asked of you?' asked with contentedness the elder Venetian merchant.

'Yes, here it is – pure gold that can be used for the making of a gold ring.' answered breathlessly the young Arturo.

'Excellent. Now my side of the bargain.'

Signore Maccarinelli handed over the key that would unlock the second chest. Just before opening the chest Arturo thought to himself with a sense of dread of the possibility of there being another chest inside the one he was opening and when his eyes spotted another smaller chest he let go of his fears with a deep and prolonged outbreath.

'The next assignment that will bring you even closer to the *desired knowledge* is the following: use your powers *of persuasion* to convince Signore Battisti to take you on as a client and arrange for him to be available to take your special order tomorrow at noon. Remember that by now he will probably resent the sight of you, but you need to **create a feeling of strong natural liking** in him for you. **Be honest, creative and confident** to achieve that liking.'

'But what if he simply refuses to do business with me or says that he is fully booked and requests that I come another day?' asked with concern Arturo.

'Then you would have wasted all of your time and efforts for nothing.' heartlessly pointed out the cunning merchant.

'I will do my best and *find a way*.' bowed honorably Arturo and left the house to make his destiny.

The Apprentice Becomes a Journeyman

Arturo left the goldsmith's place with a wide smile on his face. He was thinking how *interesting* it really was the fact that a few days ago he would be turned down by the majority of the people with higher social status he would meet when now he was getting the gist of what it takes *to be more persuasive* even though he could not consciously put his tongue on how exactly he was doing it. This time around Arturo entered the merchant's house with a *confident walk* and a *beaming smile*.

Signore Maccarinelli was very pleased when he noticed from the body language of Arturo the unspoken changes that were already taking hold of his apprentice.

'The task has been successfully completed Signore.' politely spoke Arturo while the servant confirmed the same message to his master.

'Well done. The Apprentice has become a Journeyman.' exclaimed proudly the Venetian when passing on the key to the chest to the young Arturo.

There was no surprise this time, only anticipation of a smaller treasure chest and Arturo was not disappointed for before him now lay an even smaller treasure chest and the young man was curiously ready to take on the next challenge.

'In order to earn the 4th key you have to convince the goldsmith that he needs to drop all of his current projects and devote all of his energy and skills on the one order you have for him, the details of which will be revealed to him at a later point in time.'

'But no one on Earth would drop all of their work-related matters just to devote themselves solely on one task at hand without even knowing what it will be about, unless it was somehow connected to a royalty.'

'You are on the right road. Keep in mind and **utilize the all-powerful emotion we call curiosity** to achieve this goal.'

Arturo's brain began to work in a very hurried manner trying to come up with a proper plan to help him execute successfully the advice he had just received.

Curiosity Transformed

Arturo had to struggle to convince the goldsmith for quite a while before the craftsman caved in and his *curiosity was* so *aroused* that he confirmed he would put everything on hold just to await further information from the young man. Arturo was quite proud that he was able to complete yet another assignment and as he was walking inside the merchant's house to boast with his victory he was imagining what interesting new tasks were going to follow before he could get his hands on whatever lay inside at the bottom of the chest. He did not know what it was that the chest actually contained, but he was utterly convinced that it must be of great value since he had to go through so many challenges.

'You are *progressing* very *well* and you have earned the 4th key. Here you go.' explained Signore Maccarinelli as he was handing out the key.

Arturo opened the chest hurriedly only to find another smaller box closed and locked all the while wondering how many boxes and challenges there were left for him to go through on his journey to becoming a master persuader.

'Now that you have *successfully aroused the curiosity* of Signore Battisti, you need to *transform it into* **a strong desire** to do what you ask of him. You are to instruct him to make a unique signet ring that will have a very special meaning. The design of the ring will be provided later on, but you need to *make sure you* **ignite the fire of** his **desire** before making the request for otherwise you will fail.'

Arturo *patiently* and *carefully listened to* his *teacher* and made mental notes of what he had just heard, because his experience over the last days had taught him to *keep quiet and absorb* as much as possible when a smart and wealthy man like the Signore was disclosing *valuable information.*

Painting a Picture with Words

The moment Arturo walked out of the goldsmith's workshop he breathed a deep sigh of relief. Persuading people was tremendously exhausting or at least that was the predominant thought in the young man's head.

'*Ignite the fire of his desire* – easier said than done.' was going through Arturo's mind, but he also wouldn't help but *appreciate the wise man's words* for they had assisted him in accomplishing the task.

'I must be *getting better at* this *persuasion* business since the goldsmith keeps accepting my suggestions.' Arturo thought quietly in his head as if accessing his own *growing ability to convince people* and make them see his view.

Back at the merchant's mansion Arturo reported with quiet dignity his completing the challenge that was in his way to obtaining the 5th key.

'I almost *feel proud* of you.' uttered with a devilish grin the rich merchant when addressing his apprentice.

'Here is the 5th key that is now yours.'

But this time instead of being in a hurry to open the box Arturo patiently paused for a moment, key in hand, and asked with polite scrutiny the Venetian:

'How many boxes and challenges are there left before my tuition is over?'

Instead of receiving a normal logical answer Arturo had to settle with the loud and slightly ominous laugh of Signore Maccarinelli, who appeared to be taking great pleasure out of his whole tutoring experiment. The young man then simply opened the box and found an even smaller box the sight of which annoyed him for he was fed up with all of these never-ending boxes.

'Your next goal is to persuade the goldsmith to start working passionately and without rest until he completes the signet ring upon receiving the design of the ring.'

'But his desire to help me by working on the ring is right there. I could *tell by his eyes and body language* that he was very keen on starting this project.'

'Keen – maybe, but that does not mean he cannot change his mind at any given moment. You see, you have to *make absolutely sure* that once he gets his hands on the design *he will do as you request* of him and the only way you can be certain he will do so is if you go to him again and **paint with your words the picture of** him **feeling a deep** unadulterated **sense of accomplishment** once the job is done. If you can do that, he will most certainly do as you ask.'

With a look of doubt mixed with disbelief Arturo walked out of the mansion and headed back to the goldsmith's workshop.

Almost There

This time around the goldsmith came out of his workshop accompanying Arturo and by the looks of it he was very happy from his encounter with the young man who was in turn *smiling and acting in a very friendly manner* around the elder man. Then Arturo joined the merchant's servant returned back to the rich man's mansion where the mystery of the locked box awaited.

'I believe the goldsmith is now more than *happy to cooperate* and is patiently awaiting the design of the signet ring before he can actually get to work.' Arturo repeated with *poise* that was somewhat not typical of a young man, but more commonly seen in more mature and *successful* men.

Signore Maccarinelli stood in silence for a while simply observing the metamorphosis that had taken place in the young man's behavior over the last days ever since Arturo first came to his house. Then the Venetian merchant smiled cordially as a father would smile at his son when feeling proud of his successor and he gave the young man the 6th key.

Much to the amazement of Arturo when he opened the box there was no smaller box inside it – only what looked like an ancient papyrus that was folded up into a sealed scroll. At first the young man was flabbergasted at the sight of the ancient scroll since he thought there would be another locked box that would require the completion of additional tasks. He was so taken aback that he just stood there with his jaw slightly open and eyes staring blankly at the papyrus.

'Go ahead. Open it.' urged him on the wealthy Venetian as if talking to a small boy who was afraid of the consequences if he should touch something sacred.

'No new key?' asked with lingering doubt the young Arturo.

'You have **adapted** well! The scroll is the 7th key. You just don't know it yet!'

The Star of Persuasion

Finally, Arturo mustered up the courage to open the seal and unrolled the scroll with great care and attention. Before his eyes unfolded an ancient drawing of a six-edged star with different weird looking symbols in it. Arturo did not know what to make of it. To him it just looked like an ancient cryptic drawing which carried no deeper meaning – at least not to him it didn't.

Seeing the confused expression on Arturo's face Signore Maccarinelli put his left hand over the young man's shoulder and said:

'Well, what do you think? Well worth all of the efforts, right?' uttered the merchant with a luciferian smile as if deliberately teasing the young man's ignorant mind.

'I have to be honest Signore, I expected much more for the price I had to pay for being able to see this…this…' Arturo was at a loss for words.

Signore Maccarinelli filled the whole living room there were in with his loud and some might even say wicked laughter that resonated to the very core of the young man's body and soul. After around 2 minutes of laughter the Venetian merchant ended the awkwardness of the situation by speaking gently and patiently as if explaining to a small child:

'You see, this here drawing is what you were looking for the first time you came to my house. This ancient drawing is what the knowledgeable few call 'the **Star of Persuasion**'. It is a *universally applicable system of organized and highly interconnected principles that guarantee a successful outcome* when used with the clear goal *to persuade* someone of something. The 7 symbols inside the Star are ancient runes that represent each of the **7 key principles** *involved in the successful persuasion process.* Once you *consciously learn the value of the principles* and how *they work* within the system, you will have a repeatable strategy for *persuasion* that *you* can use anywhere at any time and *get* the *results* that you want. Once you master the 7 key principles you will be able to easily *manipulate people's behavior through* your new and powerful *persuasion skills.* That is why my advice to you is to *arm yourself with patience* and an *open mind* and very soon you will have all of the knowledge you will need to be a **Master Persuader**.

Personal Power

'As you can clearly see from the drawing, the six-edged Star of Persuasion consists of two overlapping large triangles, each of which is pointing in an opposite direction – the first triangle is pointing upwards, whereas the second large triangle is pointing downwards. Let us now examine the one large triangle pointing up. This particular triangle is called the *triangle of* **Personal Power** and it symbolizes *what you need to* '**Be**' as a person to be able to *masterfully persuade* others. It represents what *is in your conscious control* to *develop within you* to '**Be**' the type of person that will be easily accepted by most and thus have the odds in your favor when it comes to *influencing others*. In order to *'Be' that person*, you need to *effectively use and master the 3 major principles* that when connected form the triangle of Personal Power and which are visually represented by each of the sides of the triangle and by a special rune at the 3 edges of the triangle. Now let us *go into greater depth on* each of *the 3 major principles*, so that you can *have a deeper understanding of the persuasion system* and how to *use it effectively*.

First Major Principle

'The first major principle from the triangle of Personal Power we will be discussing is the principal of **Rapport**, which is represented by the rune in the right angle of the large triangle.

Why Rapport? Why would Rapport be so important when it comes to influencing people? Because *people like people like themselves, they like* other *people* who are *similar to them*. That gives them *a feeling of unity*, of *being understood*, of *being appreciated*, because in their mind the *more similarities* they share with someone, the more they like that person and the *easier* it becomes *to persuade* them based on that connection that is shared.

Think of it in terms of how you *perceive* a close friend of yours – you *like* him, you probably *trust* him, otherwise he wouldn't be your friend, you like to talk to him, *share interests and experiences* with him, etc. Now think about whether it would be easier for your friend to persuade you into doing something as opposed to letting some stranger who you have no similarities with tell you what is in your best interest and just how inclined would you be to listen to them and act on their suggestions.

But let us not dwell so much on the merits of **Rapport** – instead we should *focus on gaining deep levels of Rapport* with the people we want to influence. An important point to remember is that *the cornerstone of Rapport are Similarities* – the more similarities two people have in common, the easier it is for them to be in Rapport with each other. Therefore, you have to make it a primal goal to find or create as many similarities between yourself and the person you wish to influence.

How can you do that? *By being like a chameleon* – just like the reptile changes its colors to *be in harmony* with the surroundings, you should act as a '*mirror*' and *reflect* what you see from your companion who you wish to *gain rapport* with.

There are a number of things you can *pay close attention to* and deliberately mimic when *communicating with the influencee*. You can *subtly match their posture, breathing, gestures, tone of voice, tempo, eye contact.* You can also *observe* what type of *language* and *words* they use to *express themselves* and you can *incorporate similar language patterns* when communicating with them.

What are their values, beliefs, interests? Search for them, *find* them and *be like them. Establish* in your mind what *their preferences* are and *show* them you prefer *the same things. Be a good attentive listener, lean forward a bit, and nod or shake your head to show them you are deeply interested in whatever they have to say. Show them you care and empathize with their emotional state of mind. Acknowledge their point of view, show them you understand them.* Be honest or at least try to *be perceived as honest* and caring and *create an emotional connection with them. Use the magic of your smile to show them you are open to them; give them sincere compliments and make sure you always use genuine praise* for if you are perceived as faking it, you will break the synchronicity between yourself and them. *Use their name* when addressing them and *use the magic word 'Please'* and they will appreciate you even more and when you *sincerely* want to *thank them* – do so and *use their name* so that they can feel important and enjoy your personal approach to communicating with them.

Second Major Principle

'The second major principle from the triangle of Personal Power that is crucial for *being effective in your persuasion tactics* is **Enthusiasm** and you can see it represented by the rune in the left angle of the triangle.

But what is Enthusiasm and what is its importance in the persuasion process? This ancient Greek word denotes *the presence of God in us*, it emphasizes the fact that *God's essence*, its spirit *is within us* and it is a *powerful* tool for *self-motivation* and *persuasion*.

How come? Because when you *talk and act with Enthusiasm* people listen to you more carefully and they are more prone to accepting the suggestions made by you.

Why? *Enthusiasm is an Attention catcher* – most people speak with so little vigor that nobody wants to listen to what they have to say, so when you *turn the Enthusiasm on*, your words *bypass the regular mindset* of most people and suddenly your *words become powerful* and reach and *act strongly on the hidden mind* of the people you are influencing. *Enthusiasm* even when bottled *carries powerful positive hope* and people instinctively catch on to it.

Enthusiasm presupposes that there is *something exciting, pleasant, positive* that is being conveyed and that is why the *listener's attention is automatically turned on.*

How do you *develop Enthusiasm? Act as if you are Enthusiastic and you will be Enthusiastic. Cultivate the ability to love* what *life* has to offer, *love communicating* with others and *be committed to bettering* their *lives. Develop an Obsession* within yourself; *combine Utter Determination, Passion and Faith* in yourself and your Values. You have to *be convinced to be convincing* – only then will you *speak with conviction.*

Be a high level energy person, be driven and full of excitement and remember that *your excitement can be highly contagious* and can easily flow onto the people you influence. *Believe in the words you say*, but also be smart and *keep your Enthusiasm* a lot of the times *bottled*, so that the *message* behind your words is *highly intensified* while you remain in perfect control of yourself and thus project an absolute air of Magnetism. Make no mistake – people will be drawn to you like bees to honey.

Use Enthusiasm first on yourself to motivate you to do great things; *talk to yourself with Enthusiasm* and remind yourself frequently all of the positive qualities and skills you possess and be *convinced you are a master persuader* and then *dazzle* everyone *with your* unending *Zeal*, with your unmistakable Zest.

Your *words empowered by* your *Enthusiasm* will *create emotional appeals* within the minds of the people you communicate with and do not be surprised when your emotional appeals become positively answered. Remember that it is *your tone of voice*, and *the tempo* in which you speak along with your natural manly *hand gestures* that will *carry your intensified emotions* which you want to pass onto the people you persuade, so that all of a sudden their minds catch fire from your words and automatically follow you where you want them to go.

Third Major Principle

'The third major principle that completes the triangle of Personal Power is the principle of **Alpha** and is visually represented by the rune at the top angle of the triangle. The *Alpha* principle simply *means* that you need to *be a Confident, Authoritative and Likeable* person and you will tremendously *increase* your chances of *being successful in* the field of *persuasion. Use* the power and influence of your *Attractive Physical Appearance* to your advantage *to create Likeability* and that will allow your natural or self-developed *Confidence and Authority* on a given subject to *shine through* and people will gladly accept what you suggest to them.

Improve your Posture – walk upright with more Confidence and people will not only respect you more, but also like you more and be drawn to you. When you shake hands always *have a Strong, Firm Grip* and *maintain Eye Contact* and that will add to *your being accepted as* someone *trustworthy.* When you talk to people you want to influence *use deliberately* the Power of *your Magnetic Voice* by *lowering it* when you want *to emphasize your suggestions* and you would be amazed at how effective this little technique will prove to be.

Expose your Expertise to the people you meet so that *you enhance your Credibility* in their eyes, so that they know they are talking to an *Expert,* someone who is a *figure of Authority.* Hence the power of influence of your words will be dramatically increased, at least twofold.

Know and use to your benefit the power of *Situational Status* – in every interaction there is a *figure of perceived power* whose *words and ideas are more dominant* over those of the other participants and you can *exploit that.* How? Even if you find yourself surrounded by people who have a higher social status, who are richer and usually have greater influence on certain matters than you, you can still *use the Alpha principle to take control of the situational status and redirect the conversation into your strong Domains,* you can *steer them into* the subjects *where you are the Expert* and they have no other choice but to listen to your expert opinion.

Remember also that you can *use other people's credibility* by referencing other more prominent figures' Authority on a given subject and thus you can use their perceived credibility and *piggyback on their Authority.*

When you want to *make a given point stand out* and increase the chances of its acceptance, *use the magical word 'Because'* and *use two-sided arguments* whenever you can to *create the illusion you are not biased.*

When you approach a person you want to influence always *use the power of your Smile and assume the Attitude you want from them* and more often than not they will meet your initial expectations and comply with your requests.

Develop an Attractive Personality, be someone who can be easily talked to, be *Magnetic, Persistent and Courageous* and always *accept challenges with Determination.*

The Power of the Triangle

Now that you have already familiarized yourself with the 3 major principles that form the triangle of Personal Power you need to understand that even though *every* single *one of* these *principles may be used* alone without the aid of the others *to achieve* tremendously *effective persuasive results*, the real *power of* the *triangle* is best *utilized* when the *underlying principles* are *combined, used together* to create a very sound base on which your *further persuasion actions will generate higher success rate* and you will tip the scales very much in your favor by *being Perceived as a Friend, a person with Authority that can be Trusted* and who has people's best interest at Heart. Hence *you become a person whose suggestions are very easily accepted* if you use the power of the other large triangle, of which I am about to tell you.

Creative Power

'It is now time to decipher the second large triangle from the drawing – the triangle pointing downwards that is called the triangle of **Creative Power** for it *harnesses* the powers of the *Creative Imagination to captivate the imagination of the people to be influenced and leads them to take Action*, which is the final goal of Persuasion. This triangle is all about what you need to *create deep into the hidden mind* of the influencee in order *to get them to take the action* that you want.

The 3 major principles that constitute the triangle of Creative Power are represented again by each of the 3 sides of the triangle and each rune at the edges of the triangle symbolizes the given *major principle* that *needs to be thoroughly understood, learned, memorized and* most importantly *successfully applied* over and over *again* until it *becomes part of your mental arsenal* and combines with the other major principles of the triangle of Personal Power to allow you to *be the Master Persuader* you *vehemently desire to be.*

Fourth Major Principle

'The first major principle from the triangle of Creative Power is called **Interest** and it is visually represented by the rune at the upper left angle of the second large triangle. The importance of this major principle should not be underestimated since if there is no *Interest in an idea* you are trying to *suggest* to someone then all of your effort will go to waste. That is why it is imperative that you *first use your creative skills to arouse Interest deep in the back of the influencee's mind* to the point it becomes scorching. You need to *find a way to bypass the guardian* at the gate of *the conscious mind* and *go straight to the hidden mind* where all *seeds planted and nourished carefully and creatively* will over *time sprout and lead to action*.

To do that you *first* need to *prime their mind by using pleasant associations* connected to one thing and then *guide the associations gradually* to what you really want them to think about. You need to *associate the pleasant known to the mysteriously unknown*. That will *create a fertile soil for your ideas* disguised as cleverly as the Trojan horse *to start taking deep roots* in their mind. An easy way of *guiding* them *and luring* them *into a pleasant state of mild trance* would be to *ask* them *questions* to which you know *they will answer with a single 'Yes'*. Just *keep racking up the questions* that you are almost sure they will answer with 'Yes' and soon enough their *mental guard will go down and trance will take over* and all of a sudden, the *path will become much easier* to travel.

Use simple yet cleverly disguised *Metaphors* with the *use* of *highly successful nonrational symbols* and rest assured *Logic* will have been *bypassed with ease*. Note that *metaphors* as simple as they appear to be *are a smart alternative door to the hidden mind* that *allow change to happen faster* once you are inside. They instantly *arouse the investigatory reflex* that is God-given to us and that plays such a prominent role in our lives, in our learning.

Create a sense of Mystery here and there by *telling fascinating stories* and by *choosing not to reveal too much* at once, *engage all of the senses* and you will *command their attention* and *make* even *more powerful favorable associations. Stimulate* their *curiosity* in new ways by *using taboo words* should you find an appropriate place for them and let your story *put their mind into a trance that you control. Create* your *stories as if you are sharing your own personal experience. Provide specific evidence* for your point of view. *Highlight unique benefits and exclusive information* that you reveal to them with seemingly no ulterior motive, *keep asking* them *guiding questions* to seem as if you are appealing to their logic and *appear deeply interested* in what they have to answer *by looking* them *pleasantly and politely in the eyes. Hear them out patiently* when need be and *keep exposing them to the same ideas* but dressed in new clothes *and enhance their mood by introducing novelty, danger or sex* into your stories to *keep their attention* at an all time high.

During this whole process *they* will *have grown* an even bigger *liking for you* while their hidden mind will *have grown* an extraordinary *liking for the ideas* coming from you and *your exquisite storytelling* skills.

Fifth Major Principle

The second major principle that is part of the triangle of Creative Power is called **Wanting** and it is visually represented on the drawing by the rune at the upper right angle of the large triangle. One of the main goals behind all persuasion attempts and strategies is to *create a very strong Desire* within the back of the mind of the influencee and *keep feeding that Desire until it becomes a roaring blaze* and it becomes an internal motivator for the person who is being persuaded to *quit overthinking* and instead *make a decision and act on it*. It is imperative that an irresistible *Wanting is created in their mind* that will *overrule critical thinking* if need be or supplement it and *the person* will simply *act on* their *emotionally charged desire*.

Creating a deep and unstoppable Wanting is no easy task, but it is also not that difficult either provided certain *techniques* are *used*. At the *core of* creating and using the immense power of *Wanting is to identify a* deeply rooted into the hidden mind *need* or simply create one *and then exploit it*.

All *human beings have needs* that most of the time they are *not consciously aware of* but nevertheless *they act on them*. There are some *universal human needs* that *can be taken advantage of* fairly easily *with* some *creative effort* if you first learn them by heart. *The need to love and be loved, the need to be wealthy, the need to be remembered after passing away, the need to feel important, the need to be part of a Group, the need to be congruent with one's beliefs and choices, the need to feel appreciated, the need of emotional security, the need to feel powerful, the need of approval.*

There are also *needs connected to getting away from* certain *fears* and those are: *the fear of being rejected, the fear of feeling powerless, the feat of dying, the fear of being forgotten, the fear of missing out on an opportunity. Fear is* a *powerful* factor and *driving force for human behavior* and people will go a long way just to *fill the need to avoid meeting and dealing with* these *fears*. People like to take the *easy way* out so *be smart and give it to them* on a silver platter and they will love you for it.

But, of course, the real *question of value is how do you exploit human needs to be persuasive and achieve your goals? Ask people questions to discover their personal values, identify their specific predominant needs* at a given moment *and create* a labyrinth of *mixed emotions* that will intensify the power of your words and suggestions.

Make people commit to something, regardless if it is big or small and this will *create inner tension* that will *force them to be consistent with their commitments.*

Use vivid language to *create contrast between what is and what could be,* give them *fewer choices* so that they can choose easily, *create expectations* by *being friendly and likeable* and *by creating the impression* in their mind that *you have done something for them* and *they owe you* so *that they feel pressure to reciprocate.*

Create the *illusion* that *they will miss out on an opportunity* by *creating* artificial *time constraints, show them the risk of losing* something of value if they don't take action now and *they* will *become as obedient* as sheep.

Tell them that other *people similar to them have made a certain choice* and *have benefited* from it and they will breathe out with relief and a*ccept the choice you have* so skillfully *prepared* and made available to them *by lowering your voice* at the right moment.

Obligate them to make a concession by *making them feel bad* for not accepting something else *you are offering* as *a decoy. Manage your expectations* and at the same time *expect with Confidence* that *they will agree with your proposals* and *use* disguised *verbal commands* in your language.

Deplete their Willpower by *making them think* over and answer your questions over and over so that you have an easier way to victory by *then appealing to their emotions* and by *using strong arguments* first and last.

Tease them and amplify their emotions by offering a prize worth drooling over. *Flatter them* if you have to and *feed their Greed, use their selfishness* by stating how they will benefit while others won't.

Make them feel that you care, ask for their advice to make them feel important and they will already be cooperating with you even without knowing it.

When *telling them magnetizing stories* that *evoke emotions* to *get them where you want, stop midway* and *ask* them *a question* or *talk about something else* briefly so as to *arouse an Eager Want* at the back of their mind to hear and learn the whole story and *they will* simply *feel inner pressure and* at the same time *be more open to your suggestions* since their *hidden mind* will be *jumping impatiently* like a small child *wanting to satisfy its* deep *need* to know.

Sixth Major Principle

'Now we come to the 3rd major principle of the Triangle of Creative Power which is called **Satisfaction** and it is visually represented by the rune at the bottom of the downward pointing large triangle. The main goal behind using this principle is to *give the influencee one* final yet very *important push towards taking action* by *creating a picture of the Satisfaction that awaits* them once they make the choice you want them to make and comply with your suggestions.

You need to *give them a glimpse of this enticing Satisfaction* that *they will experience if they follow your* verbal and nonverbal *lead.* You have to *immerse them into* this *imaginary world you have created* and suited just for them where *highly pleasant pictures of Self-Indulgence and Gratification are inseparable* from the *Emotional Satisfaction* they *crave to make their own and experience fully.*

You have to *create the vision of the future* in front of their eyes where what *they* already *strongly desire to attain* has been already *granted* to them- Faster, Easier, Better. *Let them enjoy the pleasures encoded in this vision* of the delightful future and *they are yours to puppeteer* as you please.

Focus your *creative efforts on* the *outcome you wish to achieve* by painting skillfully like a master painter a marvelous picture of the imaginary rewards your words promise to the influencee. Approach the *creation of the Satisfaction desired* from a perspective of *them winning while you win as well, tell them to* simply *imagine…*then *involve the other senses…make them feel good* now as they embrace the pleasure they rightfully deserve.

Promise them Prestige, promise them they will feel Important, promise them emotional security, promise them relief that will make the internal pressure go away and they will praise you for it. *Give them more than* you *promised. Give them a way to feel relieved* by *making the picture of accepting your suggestions gratifying to them* for that is the cost you make them pay after you indebted them emotionally by being so likeable and honest and since you have devoted much time, attention and interest to them and *they most certainly feel that they owe you and wish to restore their freedom from obligation.*

Let them feel part of a Group as a reward for the *desire you have* previously *built in them* for almost anyone wants strongly, *craves deeply* that illusive sense of *Belonging*, which by no accident you have pointed out as being so near their grasp if they would only do as suggested.

Flirt with the promise of attaining Love, Power, Prosperity, Immortality, Connectedness, Appreciation and they will eat out of your hand as a well-conditioned dog would. When they ask themselves the question: '*What is in it for me?*' *you offer them* a free entrance to the palace of their deep unconscious dreams called *Unity* and you will notice their relieved smile transform into a sincere, friendly, radiating smile expressing gratitude.

Master of Creation

'You have been given the secret knowledge about *the powerful major principles* that *form* the second large triangle of the *Star of Persuasion*. You would *be advised to learn well* the *major principles* and most importantly *connect them* through *practice* into a powerful structure that will make *you a Master of Creation* when it comes to *persuading people.*

Similarly, to the first large triangle the 4th, 5th and 6th principles represent very important stages in the process of Persuasion, and they can be used separately to get great results. However, their true value comes from their ability to combine with each other and form the strong geometric shape we call triangle and give the creative forces a systematic approach that will always yield the desired persuasive results.

Once you *become the Master of Creation* by harnessing the Creative Power of the second large triangle you would naturally aim at combining the powers of the conscious and hidden mind represented by the 2 large triangles to *unleash the* secret *strength of the Star of Persuasion*, but to *do that effectively* time and time again you still need to understand and properly *use the Master Key Principle* that unlocks the mystical ultimate power of the six-edged star.

Seventh Major Principle

'*The Master Key Principle* that *unites* both triangles and at the same time *enhances* their *combined powers* is of utmost importance and *should be studied and perfected* through your whole life. Underestimate it and you will reap petty results – respect its hidden strength and *make it yours* one seemingly locked door after another will start opening up to *your persuasive powers* that *will astound* the people you surround yourself with.

This *Master Key Principle is* called **Flexibility** and is visually represented by the rune at the center of **the Star of Persuasion** illustrating by its mere position the gravity of its presence, the high importance it plays in the persuasive system you have had the privilege to study up until this moment. Your knowledge would be incomplete if you were to omit this principle and rush like an amateur into applying the other major principles without properly understanding and using it in connection to the persuasive process. It allows your persuasive sword to cut through obstacles of all sorts with added sharpness where others fail.

It is no coincidence the Chinese praise the bamboo for its *unique ability to be* both strong and more importantly **flexible**. They say that when the storm comes the rigid trees, as big and strong as they are, break under the pressure while *the bamboo bends and outlasts* its relatives.

Be like the bamboo and adapt to the storms *and conquer* them. You have to *be flexible* and *increase or decrease the complexity of your message* depending on whether you want the person you are influencing to think more closely to what you are saying or if you want them to respond in a purely emotional way to your message. *Enhance their mood* in whatever way you can and *keep repeating your message* by *varying your words, your approach, by changing your story* until *you get what you want.*

Be open to receiving information from the people you influence and *be ready to make adjustments* as you *use the other 6 major principles*. Pay close attention to the influencees and be ready to *repeatedly plant suggestions* in their mind. *Repetition, repetition, repetition – use various seeds* from your bag *of suggestions* and *sow them* like a seasoned gardener would – with patience and proper care. If some of them don't germinate, *make sure you skillfully plant* plenty more and *be flexible* when watering them so that when the time comes you reap what you had originally envisioned and hoped for.

Make Adaptiveness your second nature and *subdue your inner voice of selfishness* if you have to for only the end results count and all of your *persuasion efforts have to always be goal oriented.*

The Value of a Gold Ring

It was already the break of dawn when Signore Maccarinelli finished explaining the drawing's significance and its hidden meaning. Arturo was *entranced* for God knows how long and he was *absorbing* all of *the knowledge* with the keenness of someone who longed to *be rich* at all cost and who was just given the secret that others were fully unaware of. He was the only privileged person right then and there to receive this great life-changing knowledge and he was very grateful to God for giving him the unique opportunity to get inside the Venetian's head even if for a relatively small part of his life.

'Now that *you* have come to *know the 7 major principles encoded in the Star of Persuasion* it is time for you to do one more assignment. Take this drawing and instruct the goldsmith to *engrave it* onto the signet ring without giving him any account of why you want him to do so and what the drawing really means. Once the gold signet ring is ready, bring it to my estate and from then on you will *devote* the rest of *your life to* repaying me for my revealing you the secrets behind my *success as a Master Persuader*.'

Arturo respectfully walked out of the merchant's mansion and ran like the wind to get to the goldsmith's workshop as fast as possible. All of his body was *electrified with Enthusiasm* even though he had not slept for even a minute during the whole night as the rich man had put him in this special state of mind that seemed to Arturo as if he was *flowing*.

Once he got to the goldsmith's workshop, he insisted on having the signet ring be completed in as short as time period as possible. A few days afterwards he received word that the ring was ready, and Arturo was flabbergasted at the sight of the exquisite gold signet ring as he touched the *Star of Persuasion* that had been *masterfully engraved* on it. He then hurried to the merchant's house to deliver the ring as promised, but instead of finding the rich man at his mansion, he only received a letter from the servant who had accompanied him on all of his previous assignments. Arturo opened the letter and read what looked like the merchant's handwriting:

'By now *you* already *have all the Persuasion Power you* will *need* to take you to wherever you want to go in life and *achieve all* of the *ambitious goals* I am sure you most certainly have and let this gold ring be your constant reminder of the philosophy of Persuasion as *you have learned* it through your *persistent efforts, patience and willingness to learn and grow. Use it regularly, use it well and use it with specific goals and intentions* that will allow you to *materialize your visions*, your dreams and hopes. Farewell my young friend.'

The Legacy of the Signet

'…And that is how I got this here ring that has served me well for all these years as I *became wealthy and successful through the systematic usage of the knowledge* encoded in the signet. Now the time has come for me to pass this ring and its secrets onto you, my son, so that *you* too *become prosperous, well off, successful* and live the life of your dreams by using the ring's hidden power.' Arturo spoke with tears in his eyes and a soft emotional voice as he was lying in his deathbed an old man ready to move on to the realm of the Heavenly Father after passing on his most prized possession to his beloved son, who was just a little older then he was back when he started his exciting adventure to *attain the powers of Persuasion* all those years ago that would *better* his *life* and change it almost miraculously.

Arturo's son took the gold signet ring from his father's weakening hand and embraced the old man with few tears sliding down his cheeks as rain drops on a window as he felt sadness mixed with gratitude for his father's presence in his life and for all of the valuable lessons the now old Arturo had passed onto him. No more words were spoken as father and son shared this last emotionally intense moment of Arturo's successful and happy life.

Only the gold signet ring *with the Star of Persuasion* now on the finger of Arturo's son kept glistening with a lifetime of secrets being passed on in silence to the next generation and a mysterious drawing engraved on it that would *raise questions* for many years to come.

The End